MW01109569

FLUENT JAPANESE FROM ANIME AND MANGA

How to Learn Japanese
Vocabulary, Kanji, and Grammar
The Easy and Fun Way

5.5 Edition

ERIC BODNAR

ISBN: 9781729107270

TABLE OF CONTENTS

WHAT EXACTLY IS THIS BOOK?

Half of the people who see the title to this book might be thinking to themselves, "Learn Japanese by watching anime? What a load of crap!" Such a thing certainly sounds like a crazy pipe dream that a great number of otakus share. And if you watch anime with English subtitles like most of the English speaking world does, this idea will remain merely a dream. You will not learn Japanese outside a small handful of basic words.

If you turned off the English subtitles, however, the situation would be quite different. You would be taking your first steps towards a successful Japanese learning program. Of course, this is not the only step either.

The following steps contained within this book describe a fascinating process of how anyone can teach themselves Japanese to fluency primarily through the material he or she watches and reads for fun. Inside of this book is a system that allows you to learn and never forget thousands of new words, phrases, grammar points, and kanji (漢字) that you encounter from any Japanese source of your choice. This includes anime, manga, dramas, movies, videos, music, video games, and visual novels.

Common sense says to learn Japanese mainly from traditional language learning courses and occasionally supplement it with fun things like anime and manga. Then again, you have millions of hopeful Japanese learners who begin studying and drop out when things becomes too dry and boring. This remains true even for many of the most hardcore language learners. I can personally vouch for this statement, as I dedicated four years of my life to rigorously studying Korean while living in South Korea before ultimately burning out and crashing.

I have to also confess that Japanese fiction like anime and manga does use a highly informal and caricatured version of the language. When the student understands the difference between formal and informal Japanese, however, these materials can become a very valuable resource to learn from. Fantasy Japanese contains the same vocabulary, grammar, and kanji found in all Japanese. When you combine this knowledge of Japanese politeness and formalities with the wealth of words and sentence structures that you have acquired from fun materials, you will be able to understand and talk about a large variety of different topics in Japanese whether in casual or polite language.

Perhaps you are wondering, "How long would it take to become fluent in Japanese with this system?" The answer depends on your definition of the word "fluent" as well as how much time you are willing to put into learning Japanese each day. Do you want to visit Japan and be able to hold basic five-minute conversations with strangers? Do you want to understand everything said in anime and written in manga? Do you want to fall in love with a Japanese person and converse in only Japanese? When you understand how to learn a language the fun and easy way, you will be able to smash all of those goals and go even further than you had previously imagined.

This is not your conventional language textbook that lists topics to study accompanied by new vocabulary and grammar points. You can find hundreds of those in bookstores and across the internet. Rather than dissect and explain a large hodgepodge collection of words and lines from random anime and manga that you may or may not be interested in, this book will show you a system on how to easily learn from any Japanese material of your choice.

Classes Can Be Helpful, But...

But why not just take Japanese language classes and go down the traditional path of learning a foreign language? Learning Japanese from anime and manga seems like a childish excuse to go around the hard work it really takes to learn Japanese to fluency. If you are not willing to go through years of rigorous schooling, it's easy to conclude that you are just not cut out to learn a foreign language.

Learning Japanese or any language seems so complex and difficult, but it is not. Anyone can learn a second language to fluency by using simple yet powerful language learning techniques and given enough time. This might not make any sense if you have ever suffered burnout from foreign language classes in school or at a university. They can make languages seem boring and convoluted.

Foreign language classes teach you about languages, but they do not teach you how to learn a language. After lectures and lengthy explanations, you are left to your own study devices to memorize and absorb massive amounts of information in your head. Old-fashioned study methods say to memorize vocabulary lists, do workbooks, reread old passages, and repeatedly listen to the same audio tracks found in the coursebook CDs. It can be extremely dull at times and expensive as well, but if you are studious enough, you will finish and graduate.

Even upon graduation, however, you will find that school alone does not train our minds to understand the wide variety of vocabulary, sentence structures, and seemingly blazing fast speed that native speakers use in real life. To truly reach an advanced level in a foreign language, more work is required. Classes aren't enough.

The Language Learning Bubble

Doing even a small amount of research on the topic of language learning will net you an endless list of tips and techniques, but polyglots or people who speak several languages can offer us some critical insight. Interviewers, news stories, and viral videos with millions of views make polyglots out to be language geniuses, but if we look more closely at their stories rather than their abilities, there is a deeper truth. They often struggle intensely learning their first foreign language, but something finally clicks within the gears of their minds. They learn that first one and go on to easily learn three or four or even more.

Most polyglots weren't always good at learning foreign languages. It's a skill that they develop with each new language they take on. This is why the first one can be such a challenge for everybody. Without that language learning skill and experience, trying to learn and memorize thousands of Japanese words, phrases, and grammar structures can seem like the ultimate test. And then, native speakers spit all of this out at seemingly a bazillion words a minute. It certainly sounds like a lot of hard work and study will be needed.

It's hard to argue against the value of hard work. It creates high-quality results. It pushes people to do what they need to do. It gets things done. But in the case of learning a foreign language, hard work can be very misleading.

Beginning language learners might put themselves through hell to learn all of this information. They might try to learn a language like they studied in school. Old-fashioned study methods worked back then, so why can't it work now? Rereading, rewriting, and re-listening to the same vocabulary, sentences, dialogues, and short stories is enough to ace school exams via your short-term memory, but they are not very effective means to learn and retain new language or any kind of information in the long term. They are also tedious and not very fun ways to learn.

Some exercises can be taken to frustrating levels of difficulty with the intention to learn faster. These often have the opposite effect. For instance, you could use flashcards to try to translate entire English sentences into Japanese near-verbatim. They may get you to think in Japanese, but they can be immensely stressful. Stress can be a good thing but not so much for the kind that causes you to lose motivation and take extended time off from learning.

If you have ever reached the intermediate stages of a foreign language, you might have experienced some frustration in trying to manage all of this learning. You forget words. You forget grammar rules that you have read multiple times. And of course, native speakers still talk too fast. It's quite easy to find yourself in language learning hell or eventually just quitting.

A handful of hardcore Japanese learners out there may determine that they just need to study for three or more hours a day to achieve the results they desire. I personally understand this deep and burning desire to learn, and I even used to identify myself with this level of hardcore study when learning Korean many years ago.

The truth is, however, that you don't have to study for three or more hours each day to achieve fluency. You can get fluent in Japanese with 45-90 minutes of self-study followed by a strong habit of regularly reading, watching, and listening to a variety of native Japanese materials in your free time every day. This is considerably easier to maintain in the long-term and can generate greater results through consistency.

45-90 minutes of self-study each day might not seem enough when there are thousands of words to learn. It might seem like we should spend three or more hours studying every day considering all of the phrasebooks, short stories, coursebooks, grammar books, newspaper articles, apps, and online tools available.

It's very easy to stay within a bubble of instructional materials designed for language learners. The real Japanese language and the real fun in learning it, however, lies outside of this bubble.

When you understand how to easily learn from native Japanese materials, you will understand why easy and fun wins in the end. And when you enjoy the learning process as a whole, you'll be willing to put in the extra hours of work every single day and naturally make faster progress.

If you are aiming for just a conversational level of fluency that allows you to hold basic conversations with Japanese people, you may not need to put in these extra hours of work every day. But if you want to understand everything native speakers say to each other and reach a truly high level of Japanese within a few years, you'll need to put in the hours of work each and every day.

So, What's the System?

Polyglots use a variety of methods and strategies including by not limited to learning from native materials, high frequency word learning, intensive and extensive reading, phonetic training, Anki and active recall, the Goldlist method, context-based learning, Shadowing, immersion, and frequent communication with native speakers. We will explore how you can apply these strategies to create your own self-learning program to master Japanese to fluency and beyond.

This includes an approach that I would like to share with you that combines all of these language learning techniques into one. It is by no means the standard approach that all polyglots use, but it is one application of these faster and more effective methods that will allow you to easily learn from almost any native Japanese material that you like. I enjoy it so much that I felt compelled to write this book to share this system with others who might be looking for more fun and effective ways to learn Japanese and other foreign languages.

Each chapter of this book will cover powerful language learning techniques and gradually expand on the overall main approach this book offers, but for now, here is a brief summary of that approach. Immerse yourself in any kind of Japanese material of your choice without any English subtitles or translations for roughly 20 minutes or so. This includes watching an episode of anime, reading a few manga pages, watching an episode of a drama, reading up on topics that you are highly interested in, or even playing video games in Japanese.

For this brief amount of time, very carefully listen and look for words unknown to you and that are repeated multiple times. Without stopping the video, audio, or reading, quickly jot down in a nearby notebook the unknown words that appear several times. Feel free to write down a few crucial moments that you greatly desire to understand as well. Include the video time, page number, or even in-game screenshot for later reference.

When this period of approximately 20 minutes has passed, use online dictionaries and grammar resources to quickly break down all of the words and lines on your list to learn their meanings. This will be easier to do with written materials, but for anime, we can

locate the lines using the free Japanese subtitles at
http://kitsunekko.net.

After fully learning these lines, pick up to two of them to
create very specific reading, writing, listening, and speaking
practice exercises using a free program called Anki
(*www.ankisrs.net*). These exercises will help you practice and never
forget both the lines you select and the more practical example
sentences you find in instructional materials and grammar
resources. As an alternative, you may use the Goldlist method to
practice these lines and example sentences.

As you mine a particular series or topic and regularly do these
exercises, you will come to understand it more and more over time.
You'll be actively searching for the high frequency words and
learning them. These words are the key to slowly understanding
what everyone is saying and what is going on in the story. Once
you have a strong grasp on the high frequency words, you will be
able to piece together more and more of the meaning of new
content from all sources as you first hear or see it.

So how do you get fluent from mostly just reading and
listening? For the most concrete proof of the power of extensive
reading and listening, I say look at the amazing language abilities of
the polyglots who endorse it, namely Alexander Arguelles, Luca
Lampariello, and Steve Kaufmann. There is also the overwhelming
body of research on extensive reading and listening within the
TESOL (Teaching English to Speakers of Other Languages)
community.

I am not well-versed in the study of linguistics, but this is how
I would explain it using plain English. In general, the more input
you receive and understand the more references you gain on how a
native speaker would say something. When you receive and
understand thousands of hours of input through reading and
listening, you build a massive library of references that slowly

transforms into a natural intuition of how to use the language like native speakers do. As a result, you understand nearly everything, and you can speak fluently while also sounding near-native.

Alternatively, you can also practice communicating with native speakers and receiving corrections to fill in for some of these hours. Learning via output does have its advantages. It offers a unique learning experience through active recall and corrections from native speakers. It can also be used to gauge your progress.

The decision on how much you should practice outputting Japanese will be left to you. Extroverted people, or people who gain energy from meeting and talking to other people, will find speaking and writing Japanese much easier, but introverted people may see more disadvantages than advantages here.

Will I Sound Like an Anime Character?

Yes, if you did not learn about the basic differences between casual and polite Japanese forms before attempting to communicate with native speakers. Although when we are aware of this difference, it becomes very easy to change a casual Japanese sentence found in anime and manga into its polite counterpart. How to do this will be addressed in a later chapter.

Even if you are in the beginning stages of learning Japanese, early attempts to learn from native materials are highly recommended as you progress through learning the basics. Reading, breaking down, and learning from native materials like anime, videos, and websites will be slow at first, but it will immediately connect you to the real language used by Japanese native speakers every day. This connection will be sure to bring you excitement. It will also help build an early habit of freely reading, listening to, and watching native Japanese materials without English.

Ultimately, the decision on where to start studying Japanese should be left to you, the reader. That's what makes the learning process fun and exciting! Some people want to get started by taking classes. Others want to embark on serious self-study routines, so they begin with coursebooks. And then there are folks like me who have burned out from traditional language learning methods in the past and decide to start learning Japanese primarily from anime.

Regardless of where you choose to start, this book exists to encourage all Japanese learners to incorporate native materials like anime as early as possible. In learning any language, there is no point where we become ready for native-level materials. You just have to start. In the next chapter, we will cover how you can begin learning thousands of Japanese words through anime and other native Japanese audio and video content starting today.

LEARN FROM ANIME
FROM DAY ONE

W atching anime with English subtitles is an English reading exercise with Japanese background noise. It's entertaining for sure, but you will learning nothing outside of "chotto matte" and a few other words. I have heard, and perhaps you have heard a few folks claim that they can understand 80% of Japanese dialogue after years of watching anime with English subtitles. Oh, the wonders of having the meaning automatically provided to you!

If one of your primary goals is to one day watch anime with no English subtitles, you can accomplish that goal on day one. Regardless of your Japanese ability, this is the first step that any serious Japanese learner should do starting now. You can turn them off on streaming websites like Crunchyroll, Funimation, and Netflix, but when they cannot be removed, you will need to physically block them by placing a thick sheet of paper over your computer screen.

If you have never tried removing the English subtitles and watching before, you are in for a big surprise. It's a little confusing but very exciting at the same time! With one simple change, you are no longer watching anime just for entertainment but now to also learn Japanese via your ears. Your Japanese listening comprehension has no choice but to massively improve very quickly.

If you listen carefully and attentively, you will soon start to hear the same vocabulary and grammar structures repeat over and over. You'll begin to recognize and single out these words from an otherwise stream of incomprehensible gibberish. With the end of each episode, however, you will come just a little bit closer to understanding more and more of that foreign audio stream by learning the high frequency words. With every word you learn, you'll be able to single out more new words to learn. And when you pair this practice with grammar lessons, the process speeds up exponentially.

Of course, you are going to understand very little as a beginner, but let this serve as your carrot on a stick to drive you to start and keep learning. Personally, there were many occasions I felt the need to point my finger at the screen and say, "Today I can't understand this, but one day I will."

You might be thinking to yourself, "If I can't understand anything as a beginner, what's the point? It seems like an inefficient way to learn vocabulary, and my time could be better spent studying." By all means, study for as long as you would like each day. Consider this activity as an opportunity to help you learn more Japanese even faster when you cannot study a single minute longer for the day.

No Subtitles, But How?

Begin today to reverse your deeply engraved habit of reading your anime in English. It's no easy task if you regularly watch anime. You will be tested. Our watching and reading habits have relied on English from the very start, so you will need determination and faith to fight against yourself.

Make it easier on yourself by starting with a few series that you have seen before so that you can get used to everything being in Japanese while still being able to follow the plot. Re-watch old classics like *Death Note*, *One Piece*, and *Dragon Ball Z* so that you can stay entertained while you focus heavily on the language used.

If you want to watch something new, pick a series that sounds exciting to you and try to understand just the gist. You must train yourself to be comfortable and secure not understanding everything, but this may be difficult if the plot becomes highly complex (i.e. *Re: Zero*, *Code Geass*). Trying new material and getting lost quickly is frustrating, but when you do possess something that you personally find exciting and can understand the gist, it's enough.

What counts as the gist? If you watch *Dragon Ball Z*, it's about a world where people respect the art of fighting, and Goku and his friends fight to defend Earth from invaders. If you like *Attack on Titan*, humans train to fight the terrible monsters that invade cities and eat their population. If you enjoy *One Punch Man*, it's a story of a superhero who has become too strong and dreams of a real opponent.

You may need to read a few episode summaries to catch what you missed. Some folks like to go full immersion when learning a language and read episode summaries in their target language, but I can empathize with first time language learners who already face the difficult challenge of removing English subtitles. You can read the summaries in English if you would like. Reading them in Japanese can wait until the intermediate stages.

Of course, you will miss a few plot details and many of the jokes. But if you are truly interested in the material that you are watching and desire to learn from it, you don't need to understand even a quarter of the lines or jokes to stay immersed and entertained. When you finally realize that you do not need to understand everything said and can still enjoy your favorite material, you will know victory!

Work towards building and maintaining a habit of freely listening and watching without stopping. Do not continually stop to look up words and phrases. Do not look up anything at all until this brief immersion period ends.

If English is allowed even for a few critical moments, you start to feed yourself the idea that you must understand everything to get the most out of the material. This idea, however, is not necessarily true when you consider the enjoyment you gain as you gradually notice yourself being able to understand more and more each and every day. Seeing true progress in yourself is a strong emotion. It is self-empowering.

Japanese People Do Not Talk Too Fast

You might be tempted to turn on English subtitles to help you focus on the story or relax after an intense study session, but if you choose to use them, native speakers will always talk too fast for you. This will not change until you start taking the time each and every day to practice comprehending what they mean.

There is no magical point in time where you become ready to take on native-level material without the aid of subtitles and translations. It is certainly not when you complete a full series of foreign language textbooks.

But how can you comprehend them in the beginner and intermediate stages when they use thousands of words that you do not know yet? Listening comprehension is a skill that is built through practicing with whatever vocabulary that you do know at the time and relying on context for the words that you don't know. It's similar to how you learned your first language.

You will understand the foreign language only by consistently trying to understand the foreign language. Audio from your grammar book or course is helpful, but you need every chance that you can get to build towards your listening ability. Some people like to cite that it takes roughly 10,000 hours of practice to achieve a high level of skill in anything, and this number may or may not be completely accurate. The value of consistent practice, however, is something most of us can agree on.

Despite how good it may seem for listening practice, it can be maddening watching the same episode or movie four or more times. Watch how you normally would in your native language. Once or twice is sufficient.

Double Check Your Work

After each episode ends, you will be left with a long list of scribbled words. It may not look like much at first glance, but these are the high frequency words or the key to understanding what everyone is saying. Look up as many of these words as you can in an online dictionary like Jisho (*http://jisho.org*) to learn their meaning.

Getting the correct spelling for new words can be difficult at first, but after just a few hours of learning hiragana (the most basic of the three Japanese writing systems), you'll have a much clearer understanding of how to spell new words. Online dictionaries do recognize Romaji (Japanese written in the Latin-Roman alphabet), so you can spell Japanese words using English letters for the time being.

If you are in the beginning stages of learning Japanese, don't worry about the Japanese subtitle files for now. You don't need them to start learning simple vocabulary. Some words you will be able to instantly pick up by what is on the screen and through context alone.

Understanding the exact meaning behind new words can be tricky from time to time. It can be very easy to miss the underlying tone and set expressions the Japanese use. This becomes more apparent whenever any language is translated. Perhaps you have seen the results of this in photos of funny T-shirts in Asia or in inappropriately translated signs. You wouldn't want the same thing to happen to you when you spoke or wrote Japanese, yes?

In that case, it would be a good idea to double check the English subtitles for the meaning of the new words after the episode has ended. Yet at the same time, this doesn't mean that you should use English subtitles when first watching Japanese material. This is why I recommend writing down video times for each new word for later reference. It is highly important to make sure that you completely understand what you are trying to learn before you put it into practice. Language textbooks usually provide English translations for this reason.

All this subtitle and translation talk might sound somewhat contradictory, so here's an easier way to think about it. Native-level materials are for long and extensive practice. Subtitles and translations are for short and intensive learning.

Tracking Your Progress

To help store these new words into your long-term memory, this early word-mining routine should include Anki exercises or

Goldlist method entries. It's highly recommended to create exercises or entries for each new word that you successfully learn. They will help you to not forget them and even help to track the progress you make.

Setting clear and measurable goals is the foundation behind maintaining the motivation and drive to complete any long-term goal like learning Japanese to fluency. If you're learning vocabulary, grammar, or kanji but have little to no way to track how much progress you have made, it's very easy to find yourself losing the motivation to keep going. When you have no way of judging whether or not you are improving at a skill, quitting is inevitable.

Creating Anki exercises is just one way to clearly measure the progress you have made. Watching the number of cards you accumulate over time makes your progress visible. It makes you feel that you are going in the right direction which makes it all that much easier to keep going in that direction and learning every single day.

In this book, we will look at a total of four types of Anki exercises, but in this early word-mining routine, you will only need the Production and Listening exercises. You'll be able to do the other two when you are ready to take on full sentences. You'll find these exercises located in Chapter Four.

Doing Anki exercises for just single words out of context can be somewhat monotonous, so you could even hold off on doing the reviews until you start adding sentences to Anki either from your grammar resource or elsewhere. Until then, just focus on tracking the progress you have made by accumulating more and more cards.

When you become comfortable with the routine discussed in this chapter, a typical list of 10-15 words can be learned and converted into Anki exercises within 15-20 minutes easily. When you start to go over the 20 minute mark or start getting bored, it's time to move on. There's always more anime to watch and learn from!

Best Source to Learn From?

Many folks seem very curious about what the best types of shows or genres to learn Japanese are, but the answer is simple when you realize that enjoyment and learning can go hand in hand. It's the one you actually want to watch, read, or listen to! Whatever material you want the most to immerse yourself in on a daily basis is the winner. When you learn directly from material you enjoy for the subject matter alone, you will have the daily motivation to learn for years. This sustained motivation will help you eagerly tackle any new language that you encounter elsewhere.

Constantly mixing up and switching between materials throughout the day keeps you engaged in Japanese for longer amounts of time which ultimately speeds up the rate you learn at. Considering the thousands upon thousands of words native Japanese speakers use in real life, you are going to need all the help you can get if you hope to one day understand everything they say.

If you get bored after an episode or two, try switching to a non-anime source of native Japanese like YouTube to continue your learning for the day. Of course, there are popular YouTube channels that teach Japanese like Japanesepod101, Japanese From Zero, and Nihongonomori, but these videos should be considered as study rather than native materials. After your study is finished for the day, try watching and learning from channels like Fischer's, 兄者弟者 (2Bro), and はじめしゃちょー (President Hajime).

You literally have an entire Japanese speaking world to explore. Be sure to check out Niconico (*http://www.nicovideo.jp*) when you are in need of new Japanese media to sink your teeth into. And if you are into live streaming services like Twitch, you may enjoy crawling through OPENREC.tv (*https://www.openrec.tv*). And if you want to try to learn from Japanese TV shows and dramas, Netflix offers a fair selection to choose from.

Japanese Subtitles

While Japanese subtitles are extremely helpful to learning key moments from video materials, it's poison to your listening comprehension ability. Sadly, Japanese subtitles don't come equipped with people you encounter in Japan. So it's highly recommended to turn these subtitles off, too, while watching.

Listening comprehension is arguably the weakest skill of the average adult language learner, for most instruction of the target language is provided through text or explanations in the learner's native tongue. Classrooms and even audio language courses simply do not provide the thousands of hours of practice necessary to understand native speakers out in the everyday world.

Most of us don't have a Japanese mommy or daddy to speak to us every day for 8-12 hours for 10+ years. You can pay tutors to do just that, but that becomes expensive to do every day for even one hour a day. Without these adult native speakers constantly around, your Japanese ears will remain incredibly weak. You have a lot of catching up to do.

Learning Japanese from music via song lyrics, however, could be one reasonable exception to this rule. Singing the correct lyrics is already a difficult endeavor in our native language, and mishearing lyrics is just as common as it is funny. Start with the lyrics and make it a game to work your way towards relying less and less on them. If you don't want to sing and would rather just listen, this won't do at all. You are missing a huge opportunity to improve your pronunciation, learn language through mimicry, and have quite a lot of fun.

KANJI AND GRAMMAR
ARE EASY

---

arly attempts to learn from native Japanese materials like anime are absolutely encouraged for beginners, yet without learning the basics of Japanese as you progress, your language ability will be very limited. You're highly likely to have some trouble getting around Japan if you can't read or write Japanese. Without knowing the differences between polite and casual speech, you could come off as a little arrogant to Japanese people. They will most likely find it very difficult to understand what you want to say if you have no knowledge of Japanese pitch accent or intonation.

The good news is that all of the above is easily learn-able. With smart language learning techniques, it's also fun. And it's only a matter of time until it all becomes second nature.

This chapter will be a collection of language learning strategies that you may find useful if you are struggling with learning the basic building blocks of Japanese. These strategies aim to save you time and from frustration in learning Japanese kana, kanji, honorifics, grammar, phrases, and pitch accent.

Start with whatever excites you the most. A few people will study only phonetics at first for months and perhaps even a full year or two with the goal of sounding as native-like as possible. In the case of author James Heisig, he decided to first tackle the problem of remembering the meaning and writing of the

Japanese kanji characters before learning anything else. Others may be looking for a more guided approach, so they use websites and apps like Duolingo.

In the age of technology, quick internet searches, and YouTube, it has become even easier to learn anything including a foreign language without classroom instruction or even a single textbook. For the sake of streamlined learning, however, I would recommend a coursebook or textbook but a maximum of just one. A high-quality coursebook does provide well-rounded introductions to foreign languages, solid grammar explanations, and a wealth of words, phrases, and sentences to create Anki exercises with.

Coursebooks and other Japanese learning resources provide a safe and sheltered source for learning, yet it is important to escape this language learning bubble as early as possible. Outside of that is where the true language and culture lie. There may be a set of six textbooks to learn Japanese, but you may only need the first one before you are able to learn primarily from material made for native speakers. Following your coursebook and Anki study time with a strong habit of reading and listening to native materials daily can make that happen.

Put in the Hours Every Day

Doing Japanese three times a week for 30 minutes will deliver mediocre results. By limiting yourself to just three times a week, you will struggle to understand and communicate in Japanese for 20 years before you are able to reach any level of fluency.

Creating and maintaining a daily habit of language learning will be one of your first challenges. Focus on not breaking the daily habit at all costs. Consistency builds habits. Once that consistency and priority in learning Japanese has been established, you can build upon your daily routine by incorporating more reading and listening to native Japanese.

Languages are not just knowledge but also a set of skills our eyes, ears, mouths, hands, and brains must practice daily in order to achieve fluency. If you only end up with 30 minutes of Japanese learning time after a day full of chaos, so be it. You may not learn much for that day, but these small yet consistent actions do build towards new habits that will enable you to make this major lifestyle change.

Managing only 30 minutes of Japanese learning time on a single day is not going to slow you down too much, but consistently doing only 30 minutes each day will. This habit should not be taken lightly if you truly want to reach a high level of Japanese. You're trying to learn an entirely new foreign language and culture and not just how to fold your laundry. Show up every single day and put in the hours of work through study and reading and listening to native Japanese.

Japanese Kana

Let's start with the basics. Japanese has three writing systems: ひらがな (hiragana), カタカナ (katakana), and 漢字 (kanji). Romaji is not Japanese and relying on it for too long will place a severe handicap upon your reading ability that is extremely difficult to undo. If you haven't already learned kana (hiragana and katakana), you may want to make that one of your first priorities. Fortunately, reading and writing these characters is an easy task for most folks.

I highly encourage you to use a resource that teaches the characters with the help of mnemonics and in the context of vocabulary words. You can find one such resource here — *https://www.youtube.com/watch?v=6p9Il_j0zjc.* You can also find this video by searching YouTube for "Learn ALL Hiragana in 1 Hour —How to Write and Read Japanese".

Training yourself to write the kana from memory with the help of mnemonics will help to prepare you to take on the kanji. Writing characters over and over and repetitive reading drills will work for the kana, but they are highly ineffective ways to learn the kanji. There are only 92 kana characters, but there are 2,000+ general-use kanji characters that you should take this opportunity to prepare yourself for.

Common Pronunciation Mistakes

When we learn to speak new languages like Japanese, we unconsciously and unknowingly project and apply the phonetic rules from our first language. We are hardwired to the speech patterns of our native language after speaking it for so long. The good news is that we can correct most of these mistakes with just a little bit of phonetic training. Let's start with a few that can easily be corrected right now.

The Japanese ふ sound is romanized as "fu" or "hu", but the actual sound doesn't exist in English. In phonetics, this [ɸ] sound is called the voiceless bilabial fricative, but as complicated as the phonetic names to these sounds are, learning to reproduce them is not. Start by saying the English word "foo" (like in 'food'). Notice how your upper teeth comes in contact with your lower lips. Now just try to make the same sound but without making your upper teeth and lower lips touch. That is ふ.

Next, we have the Japanese し, ち, and じ sounds. The Japanese し sound is very similar to saying the English word "she", but your lips are much more relaxed and do not stretch out at all when making this [ɕ] (voiceless alveolo-palatal fricative) sound. The very same applies to the Japanese ち sound. It's like saying "chi" but with relaxed lips and cheeks. This also covers the Japanese sound じ, which is phonetically known as [ʑ] (voiced alveolo-palatal fricative). It's the relaxed version of "gee" (like in "Jesus').

Japanese people have quite the hurdle to jump in learning the English 'L' and 'R', but fortunately for you, the Japanese 'R' [ɾ] (alveolar tap) already exists in English. It's found in the middle of words like "butter", "ladder", and "putter". From there, it's simply a matter of starting syllables with this sound to produce the Japanese sounds ら, り, る, れ, and ろ.

Kanji Are NOT Impossible!

Learning the writing, meaning, readings to each kanji looks hopeless at first sight, but creative mnemonics can make this task not just manageable but incredibly fun and easy. Professor James Heisig, author of "Remembering the Kanji", teaches us that our imaginative memory is much stronger than our visual memory. Rather than trying to memorize mundane collections of pen strokes, reading and writing kanji can be a fun exercise in recalling highly memorable, imaginative, and silly mnemonic stories.

Heisig's book is highly recommended as a supplementary resource and not by just me but a large portion of the Japanese learning community. The book will teach you how to write any kanji perfectly by tying its primary meaning to a single unique word in English. From this keyword, you can recall its specific mnemonic story which provides a mental map of instructions on how to write the kanji from memory.

When you practice starting from English keywords to write the corresponding kanji, reading them becomes effortless. The Heisig method tackles both reading and writing in one fell swoop.

The author's instructions are the key to success with these kanji mnemonics. Whenever you first learn a new character, take just a minute to close your eyes and retell yourself its mnemonic story. Then, write the kanji. Don't try to remember what each character looks like. Don't just copy it into your notebook. Try to let your imagination do the bulk of the work.

If you write the characters even just once in this fashion as you learn them, you will know the characters at a much deeper and even personal level. This alone can severely cut down your kanji review time.

You may not see the power of mnemonics until you start the review process and have to recall stories when your visual memory fails you. This method might help you even gain a love and appreciation for the kanji.

A later chapter will expand on how to balance learning from these kanji resources and native-level reading materials.

Casual and Polite Language

The majority of characters in anime and manga use casual language with the exception of a few characters who speak mostly in the polite language. You can take almost anything you see or hear in fictional Japanese and make it polite. For example, you will hear **ありがとう** (meaning "thank you") in anime and manga frequently, but you will need to say **ありがとうございます** when speaking politely. If you have not learned kana yet, you may need to revisit this section at a later time.

Polite language should be used when talking with people you do not know well, people older than yourself, or people in a higher position of power than yourself. Informal language should be only used with close friends, people you know who are the same age as you or younger, or those in a similar social standing as yourself. So **ありがとう** can be used with family, friends, peers, and children. And **ありがとうございます** should be used with strangers, older folk, and your boss.

Let's take a quick look at how some casual sentence ending particles can be replaced with polite counterparts. Very common particles like **よ** and **ね** change to **ですよ** and **ですね** respectively. When Japanese people get excited about something, you will hear **ぜ** and **ぞ** in casual speech, and these can be swapped with **ます**, **ですよね**, or **ましょう** depending on the context. Casual masculine speech forms like **だろう** could be substituted with **です** or **でしょう** and be used by both sexes. This also includes casual feminine particles like **かしら**, which might be replaced by the gender-neutral **かもしれない** in polite speech.

Your initial coursebook should cover the basics of polite speech, but if you are ever unsure whether certain language is casual or polite, look it up in an online dictionary or with an internet search. If a clear answer is not found, you can also ask a native speaker directly.

Some folks might be worried that they will accidentally learn anime catchphrases, but a basic grammar primer and hundreds of hours of listening to anime without subtitles will help you easily spot catchphrases used by characters like Naruto. They will *immediately* stand out to your ears.

People love to knock down the idea of learning Japanese from cartoons, and there is some merit that we should give in respect to the rude and offensive language used. We will need to take some precaution. Once we understand these offensive words found in fantasy Japanese, however, we will be able to look past it and see the gold mine of vocabulary, kanji, and sentences used by native Japanese speakers for native Japanese speakers. There is an endless supply of useful vocabulary, phrases, and sentences that we can learn from.

There are rude words and phrases that should not be used in polite speech even with polite forms. In the next section, you will find some words that commonly appear in anime and manga that can be taken to be very offensive.

For example, do not use the word **あなた** meaning "you". In English, it's very common to use pronouns like you, I, and we, but this is not the case in polite Japanese.

Despite how often you hear and see **あなた** in fantasy Japanese and even as a generic subject in example sentences, this word is unnatural in daily conversation. It can even be taken as cold or condescending. This is especially true towards folks the same age as yourself or older or to people in positions of higher power. This word is sometimes used, however, by older couples to address each other. But in general, it's much more natural to speak without this pronoun and call folks by their last name plus the suffix **ーさん** or their job title if you work together.

Keep in mind that this is not a complete list of Japanese slang and offensive words but a list of the most common ones that appear in native materials like anime and manga. There are many others of course, but you will learn and recognize them in time.

Potentially Offensive Japanese Words:

お前 (おまえ) --- you (very informal)

手前 (てめえ) --- you (also very informal)

貴様 (きさま) --- you son a bitch

野郎 (やろう) --- bastard

奴 (やつ) --- that person/thing (used with very close friends only)

コイツ (こいつ) --- this guy (used with very close friends only)

あいつ --- that guy (used with very close friends only)

-やがる --- freaking (as in "I freaking went to the store")

くそ --- Damn!

畜生 (ちくしょう) --- Damn it!

馬鹿 (ばか) --- stupid

馬鹿野郎 (ばかやろう) --- idiot

黙れ< (だまれ) --- shut your mouth

煩い (うるさい) --- shut up

最低 (さいてい) --- horrible / disgusting / the worst

いい加減に (いいかげんに) --- cut it out

ふざけるな --- stop screwing around

ガキ (がき) --- brat

チビ (ちび) --- little person (sensitive word)

Japanese Pitch Accent

Japanese pitch accent is completely overlooked and neglected by the majority of Japanese language learners. I was guilty of this myself for the first three years of my study, and as a result, I spoke with a very heavy American accent.

This topic is only briefly mentioned in most Japanese learning materials, but its importance should not be underestimated. If you want to lose your foreign accent and have a decent shot at sounding like a Japanese person, studying pitch accent is a must. It's the core to basic Japanese pronunciation and intonation. Pitch accent makes all the difference between unnatural and natural sounding Japanese.

Spoken Japanese alternates between low and high pitch sounds, and it is very difficult to detect and mimic without prior knowledge. Spoken English does the same thing, yet we add stress and volume to our sounds. Japanese does not.

Every single Japanese word has high and low sounds, and every single word experiences a change in pitch in between the first and second phonetic sounds (moras). If the first mora starts high, the next mora will be low. And if the first mora starts low, the next mora will be high. Even words with a single mora start high or low and then change when a grammar particle like が or は is added. For example, 木 (き), the Japanese word for tree, has no initial pitch accent, but 木が starts high and ends low.

Having to learn every single pitch accent for every single Japanese word does sound overwhelming at first, but there are many shortcuts you can take to simplify this problem. First, just focus on learning the pitch accents for the most basic and common Japanese words like 私 (わたし), the polite Japanese word for I / me. Native English speakers often over-emphasize the first mora and say "Watashi wa...", but 私 actually starts low and ends high.

Getting the pitch accent right for these basic and common words will immediately improve your accent overnight. You'll even begin to see some helpful patterns emerge if you stay patient. For instance, これ (this), それ (that), and あれ (that over there) all start low and end high.

You can check the pitch accent of any new word you learn using a free tool called Suzuki-kun (*http://www.gavo.t.u-tokyo.ac.jp/ojad/eng/phrasing/index*). Simply copy, paste, and click analyze to get a graph of the pitch accent. Single words, short phrases, and simple sentences work best, as longer sentences tend to not be completely accurate. Don't worry about the settings, as the default ones are more than good enough. This tool can even generate an audio file of an automated speaker demonstrating the correct pitch accent.

For more information about Japanese pitch accent, I highly recommend Dogen's Japanese Phonetics series on Patreon (*https://www.patreon.com/dogen*). He offers a solid introductory video course on pitch accent without going too much into the phonetic and linguistic jargon. It's very difficult to memorize all the pitch accent patterns he throws at you, but the Anki exercises covered in the next chapter can provide some assistance.

Stop Taking Textbooks So Seriously!

Your textbook should be your loyal and faithful servant and not the other way around. Do not let it become your master. What I mean is that it should not take up the majority of your study and learning time.

Let these books briefly serve you, and then, dismiss them. Seek five minute explanations for new language and grammar structures. Don't bother with drills and grammatical exercises if they don't interest you. Don't write words out over and over. Don't bore yourself with the comprehension questions in the book. Understand the gist and get out of there! A daily habit of reading and listening to native Japanese materials as well as Anki exercises will make sure that you receive more than enough practice.

Use your coursebook time to feed Anki the new information that you wish to practice. New vocabulary words, phrases, kanji, grammar structures, verb conjugations, monologues, dialogues, and long passages can be divided and conquered through a variety of Anki exercises.

It's not necessary to turn every new word and sentence into an Anki card, or otherwise, you might fall asleep before you make it to the next chapter! Do what you can until you get bored and simply move on. While coursebooks and Anki are helpful tools, they are not as important as reading and listening to native Japanese materials.

A Most Common Mistake

There will be quite a lot of learning activities that require a bit of balancing: learning from your textbook and primary courses, learning directly from multiple native Japanese materials, Anki practice, and communicating with native speakers in Japanese (optional). Cycle between multiple activities every day and try not to get caught up in focusing on just one. This cycle and variety in your daily routine will be sure to maximize your attention span and help you absorb even more Japanese.

Here's where beginning language learners make the most common mistake. It's a mistake that often puts an early end to many hopeful newcomers in learning a new language. There is no need to finish your initial course or coursebook before you try learning directly from native Japanese materials. You don't even need to finish the book or course at all! Learn what you can from it until you get bored.

Boredom is our brain's way of telling us that we are going to burn out if we continue to push ourselves to learn from the same material day after day. Our brains are smart that way. It knows when something is no longer working. Resistance to learning doesn't mean that we are stupid or lazy. It means to stop and do something different.

It's so easy to blame ourselves for getting bored because we might feel that we should learn all this serious material before we get to learn from fun materials. That line of thinking, however, is not true at all. Learning from fun materials is the key to never getting bored and quitting.

Hop around materials as you personally see fit! Jump between several courses and your true interests in the Japanese language. Jump between learning kana, kanji, pitch accent, your coursebook, and anime of course. Whatever you truly desire to learn from is where you should go next. Listening to and following that desire is what keeps you learning. That's the secret to wanting to learn and improve each and every day.

When you personally make the connection between what you are studying from instructional materials to what you see in native materials, that will boost your motivation more than almost anything else. That is how you can eventually conquer all the serious Japanese you feel that you should learn.

Early Output or No?

The choice of whether or not to include output and communication with native speakers early on in the language learning process will be left to you. This is somewhat of a hot topic currently being debated within the polyglot community and is worthy of its own book, but here is a summary of the main issue boiled down into a single sentence. Early output offers a unique way to learn through experimentation and corrections, yet at the same time, we run the risk of building unnatural speaking habits early on since it's difficult for native speakers to correct every single one of our mistakes.

Ultimately, you must decide when exactly to begin incorporating output practice. If you are seeking immediate results and would like to communicate with Japanese people as soon as possible, speaking or writing Japanese every single day becomes a natural priority. Some polyglots go as far as to speak with tutors from day one in only the target language, and others have demonstrated amazing results using mostly input-based approaches. Either way, we will discuss how to get into contact with native speakers and receive corrections in the last chapter.

How About More Advanced Textbooks?

You might feel that you haven't mastered the basics after one textbook, and this feeling may definitely reflect some truth. And what about the everyday things in life in Japan: paying bills, renting an apartment, going to the bank, and working at a company? If you would like to live and work abroad one day, a certain set of vocabulary and phrases is going to be needed. You may even wish to purchase an additional coursebook to make sure that you don't sound like another helpless weeb. Go for it.

Some dedicated language learners find a series of coursebooks and textbooks to be interesting because progression and the learning process itself can be exciting. Every chapter brings new grammar structures that allow the learner to express larger and larger ideas. The beginning months can be highly stimulating and intriguing since everything is new, and coursebooks present these new ideas and grammar structures in a way that is easy to understand.

Some of those who have reached the intermediate stages of learning a foreign language, however, can testify to what eventually follows after the first few textbooks are completed. We realize that we still struggle to understand most native material, so we buy more advanced books covering more grammar, phrases, and idioms. We go harder in our learning routine and study for more than three hours per day. These advanced grammar explanations are now long-winded, and new language can be highly situational. And there's always more vocabulary to memorize. The first few thousand came easy with some effort, but now suddenly there's 30,000 that we feel that we are expected to know!

"Fun? There's no time for that. I have to learn more!", may be the last words of your motivation before it disappears. It's so easy to become trapped and confined within a bubble of language learning materials. Learning can unknowingly become stale, boring, and inefficient for months and even years before you eventually quit all together.

An Alternative Course

Let's use these advanced resources as references to look up any new or unfamiliar language structures when we encounter them in native Japanese materials. Wouldn't it be nice to quickly drop in, understand the gist of the target word or structure, and be done with these resources? Lengthy grammar explanations can easily be forgotten, yet a large context from a story that we truly care about can burn in our memory for years. That's the power of context.

Make native materials your new textbook. Switch your primary source of learning to Japanese dramas, anime, manga, visual novels, music, or whatever got you interested in the language in the first place. It's not a farfetched idea if you have traveled to a non-English speaking country before and met one of the millions of people who have learned English by watching American TV, dramas, and movies.

You might not even need any advanced Japanese textbook. Online dictionaries can provide the basic meaning to an overwhelming majority of words and phrases and give plenty of example sentences. If more explanation is desired, internet searches for target sentence structures in Japanese and English will reveal resources that can provide accurate descriptions to most structures. And when you want to cut corners and save time, subtitles and translations in both languages can speed things up.

HOW TO MAKE IT STICK

Simply encountering and looking up a new word, grammar structure, or kanji does not mean that we have truly learned it. It may reside in our short-term memory for a short while, but we simply forget things as humans. If we can't recall a word while speaking or recognize it during a conversation, we haven't truly learned it yet. We acquire words and all of their connotations for good by encountering them over and over in a wide variety of contexts.

In general, rereading and rewriting new vocabulary, phrases, and sentences in mass is not very efficient in helping us retain that new information. It also happens to be incredibly boring and tedious.

I found this out the hard way. I used to torture myself with this kind of review for hours on a daily basis back in my Korean learning days. And of course, this excessive emphasis on review led to my eventual crash and burnout as it commonly does with many language learners.

Anki aims to simplify and consolidate our review time by combining intelligent flashcard exercises with a Spaced Repetition System (SRS). The SRS is designed to test us on information at intervals just before we are likely to forget.

Anki is just one way to review, but it is not the only way. The Goldlist method is another way. Review can also be done through more reading and listening to native materials or even by communicating with native speakers.

I believe what is most important about Anki is its ability to clearly measure and track the progress you have made in the beginning and early intermediate levels. At these levels, it's difficult to see visible and clear progress when trying to learn from native materials or when trying to express your exact thoughts with native speakers. In fact, it's very easy to get frustrated, and your efforts to learn here can feel like trying to drain a lake using only a single cup as a tool.

But with Anki, you can see clear and consistent progress in the amount of cards you make and in your ability to successfully recall things that you have learned. The feeling of clear and consistent progress helps you to keep learning and especially on the days you really don't feel like it.

Some language learners out there hold a strong dislike for Anki and flashcards, and I can understand why. They can get really boring really fast. Flashcards can remind us of the useless facts that we were required to memorize for school tests and forgot just a week later.

Basic flashcards alone are unable to hold our attention for very long, but that's the thing. It's just one amongst many review exercises. Problems arise when you do nothing but basic flashcards in Anki. Additional problems begin to accumulate when you do excessive amounts of review, but we will cover that issue in the last two chapters. First, let's just focus on the types of exercises themselves.

This chapter will introduce Production, Cloze, Listening, and Shadowing exercises in an attempt to make Anki a more viable option for more people by adding some spice and variety to traditional flashcards. These four exercise types will help you to practice any new vocabulary, phrases, grammar, and kanji that you wish to master. When you combine these exercises in Anki, you get a single activity where you can practice reading, writing, speaking, and listening to Japanese all at once.

Anki does not come with any pre-made decks for Japanese or anything for that matter. Although you can download user-created decks for free, it's highly recommended by an overwhelming majority of the language learning community to create your own decks. Without that personal connection you get from making your own exercises using the material you are studying, you'll lose interest fast.

Your personal decks can be made using instructional materials, native Japanese materials, and also what you personally need the most help with. When you put the effort into creating the deck, the exercises come to life in a way. Combining these four exercise types alongside a wide variety of Japanese sources will help to keep you on your toes each review session. You will never know what is coming up next.

Production

Let's start with a very basic exercise but one with an important purpose. Simply, you'll be given a word in English or a picture and have to say aloud the equivalent word in Japanese. That's it. Yet it should not be underestimated because of its simplicity. When you have a strong mix and balance of other exercises to go with this simple one, this exercise is perfect.

Production exercises have two very important uses. First, our ability to speak a new language is greatly enhanced just by being able to recall thousands of very simple and straightforward words and phrases with lightning speed and little to no trouble. We need to know how to quickly say things like 青 (blue), 丸 (circle),

運転手 (bus driver), 牛乳パック (milk carton), 喉が痛い (to have a sore throat), 皿を洗う (to wash the dishes), 電気を消す (to turn on the lights), and コンセントに差す (to plug in). That's where Production exercises in the right quantity can help you.

If you can't remember a word or phrase after five seconds, just retest it. Don't strain yourself in order to recall it. And don't try to push it into your mind in order to remember it next time. Those are short-term memory tactics. Some words and phrases require a single test to learn while others may require six, seven, eight, or even more retests over a period of several months to make it into our long-term memory.

The second use of this exercise is to practice good pitch accent and pronunciation. Pay special attention to properly producing each sound like a native speaker would. This special attention makes all the difference between a thick foreign accent and an authentic Japanese accent.

For instance, when you see "decay" on the front side of this flashcard exercise, instead of just quickly muttering "fuhai" to yourself, practice saying it aloud with proper pitch accent and pronunciation. Really focus on starting with a low pitch and gradually raising it to a high pitch like Japanese people do when they say 腐敗. Take the extra two seconds to make sure you are properly producing the [ɸ] sound.

Short and Sweet

What if you reverse the order and put Japanese on the front and English on the back? This would change the Production exercise to a reading and translation exercise, which is useful, yet you will get plenty of reading from the Cloze and Shadowing exercises. Additionally, the Listening exercises will give you a more interesting way to test your recognition of these words.

Putting just the English word on the front side of this flashcard saves a lot of time, or you could also put an image representing the word here to provide some context. The choice is yours. Abstract words like 気晴らし (a distraction) and 決断 (a decision) will be much more difficult to find proper images for, so the English word might be the easiest option here.

It's highly recommended to stick with just single words and small phrases. If you put full English sentences on the front and try to recall them verbatim in the target language, you can potentially put yourself through language learning hell. The possibility of all kinds of synonyms and different translations makes it frustrating. Too many questions can come up when you think of an answer that seems correct yet is different from the answer on the back. You might find yourself irritated wondering whether or not the answer that you came up with is correct or not. It's tedious and not a very pleasant learning experience.

Let's say you want to learn from a basic sentence like "冷蔵庫のドアを開いたらリンゴが落ちた" which means "when I opened the door of the refrigerator, the apple fell out." Instead of trying to memorize the full sentence, use these basic Production exercises to help you memorize single words like 冷蔵庫(refrigerator), ドア (door), 開く (to open), りんご (apple), and 落ちた (fell). Make exercises for very short phrases like 冷蔵庫のドア (refrigerator door) and リンゴが落ちた (the apple fell).

Cloze

If you are a fan of learning through context, Cloze is the exercise for you. And it can be used to learn much more than just single words and phrases.

On the front side of these cards, you will be presented with a small context (a sentence or a few sentences) that you have learned beforehand except that one small piece will be missing. The objective is to figure out what is missing based on the surrounding context and write the answer in your notebook. That missing piece can be a single kanji character, a word, or a piece of grammar. This simple exercise will require you to think in Japanese while you strengthen your reading and writing skills with virtually no stress.

Context makes these challenges interesting and fun. Test writing new kanji in context. Test new vocabulary and phrases one kanji at a time. Test for even the easy kanji within new vocabulary and expressions. Test for grammar structures like 〜たりする. And test for correct grammar particle usage which can be so oddly specific and tricky at times (e.g. に vs. で, が vs. は).

There is no need to write any single kanji more than once. There is no need to test for large amounts of missing information. There is no need to copy whole sentences down in our notebook. There is no need to memorize these sentences to recite later.

Instead, you will see all of the new vocabulary, kanji, and grammar points again and again in the variety of Anki cards that you can make for each context. While you are testing yourself on something small, you will still need to use the other information to help you determine the missing piece.

To create Cloze cards in Anki, first make sure 'Cloze' is selected at the top left corner when adding cards. Now, place your text in the 'Front' box. Next, highlight the single kanji character, word, or piece of grammar that you wish to practice and press the "[...]" button. Click 'Add' and you are all finished.

One Kanji Max

I would like to share a personal anecdote to better illustrate this idea. I used to test myself on two or more kanji at a time many years ago. I believed that if the combined kanji were somewhat known and simple enough, I should be able to recall them with little effort. Then one day, a Cloze exercise came up during my Anki session, and I instantly recognized outer space (宇宙) was missing. I quickly picked up my pen only to become hesitant moments later.

I had seen the word *hundreds* of times on paper and could say the Japanese word aloud (うちゅう), but I could not write it. I knew that it consisted of two kanji: one for "outer space" and one for "mid-air". Yet was that the right order? Was it "mid-air" and then "outer space"? Unable to answer my own question, my confidence shriveled, and I suddenly could not recall how to write either kanji! I could instantly recognize it if it were written somewhere, but how could I not write these two very simple kanji?

A large light bulb moment suddenly struck me while my frustration was bubbling up inside. If I tested just one kanji at a time, I would actually have much more fun and enjoyment compared to now. It would make things so much easier, and I would still be learning how to read and write thousands of kanji. When the learning process is made easier, it's more fun, and as a result, I would naturally want to do more of it each and every single day.

Test only one kanji at a time. When you test for two or more kanji at the same time, you give yourself far less context to work with. There might not be enough context to be able to figure out what exactly is missing. First, you have to remember the exact new word or phrase missing in the sentence from all the possible synonyms. This includes what kanji make up the new piece of language and the correct order of the characters. Then, you would have to remember how to write each kanji. That is far too much!

While you should only test yourself on one kanji, you can choose to include some kana for vocabulary that require it. For example, if the kanji is used in an adjective, you can test for your ability to recall the kanji and also whether it is an -i adjective or -na adjective like in 安い (cheap). Of course, you may also make Cloze cards to test yourself on vocabulary words that are written in kana like たんこぶ (a bump / lump).

Listening

Stop passively listening over and over to the same conversations and same short stories in Japanese and expecting to learn more. It's a big waste of time. Instead, test your listening one word, phrase, and sentence at a time.

The Listening exercises are simply listening more or less, but text-to-speech programs can completely change how we practice listening comprehension these days. There exists a way to take words, phrases, and sentences from any source at all and generate free audio recordings of an automated native speaker saying those words. These audio recordings can then be placed inside of Anki to make listening the easiest and most fun language skill to practice.

Amazing nor astounding does not even begin to describe this awesome power now available to everybody. Your ears are going to beat the panties off of most Japanese learners.

The front side to these flashcard exercises will be blank, but an audio file of two to three seconds in length will play. It's your task to either think or say aloud the equivalent in your native tongue. You either get it or don't within the next three seconds. It's a very simple and effective exercise in training your ears to instantly decode the meaning of spoken words just like you can in your first language. The Cloze exercises do take a little time and effort to figure out, but the Listening and Production cards help break up the monotony with on the spot lightning round challenges.

On the back side of these flashcard exercises, I recommend putting the English translation and the Japanese transcription of the audio file to check for complete comprehension. Cloze and potentially Production can be done in only Japanese, but using English here is perhaps the simplest way to check if you fully understand the meaning behind the words. Freely listening to and reading native Japanese material without English is essential to fluency, yet this is another case where you may learn more by including your native language.

Unlike the Production cards, however, you can test your comprehension of sentences in full one by one. Undoubtedly, there are going to be some synonyms when translating full sentences from one language to another, but it takes much less effort to translate sentences from Japanese to your native language. Try it yourself and see how fast they go by.

Shadowing

I will admit that this last exercise requires a few hoops to jump through to setup inside of Anki. I understand that you may not be willing to acquire source files and extract audio from them. If it is too much of a hassle, you can skip this exercise. It is optional.

The Shadowing technique is one way to put more Japanese on our tongues. It was developed and popularized by hyperpolyglot Alexander Arguelles, and in its original form, it requires long dialogues and short stories as well as adequate space to march back and forth in. I would like to include a somewhat condensed form of Shadowing that can be done inside of Anki.

It's as simple as repeating aloud what you are hearing as you hear it to the best of your ability. In Shadowing, you do not repeat after the audio file when it has stopped, but instead, you talk on top of it continuously for the entire recording. Two or three attempts each time will be good enough.

There are three types of Shadowing that can be done: Shadowing with no text (Blind Shadowing), Shadowing with the English translation, and Shadowing with the transcription in the foreign language. All of them will include audio in the foreign language. To create these exercises in Anki, simply just place the text and audio in the 'Front' box and leave the 'Back' box empty.

When no text is present, you are focusing solely on the sounds of the language and reproducing them with your mouth. Even though you may have little to no idea what you are saying, the point is to listen intensively and get used to the feeling of speaking new sounds and words.

When Shadowing with the English translation, you are still repeating what you hear but now with complete understanding. Don't worry about the exact meaning of each word and how they are phrased but instead just focus on the overall meaning here.

And when Shadowing with the Japanese transcription, you are listening, speaking, and reading in Japanese all at once. Use the text to help you pronounce all the words while still focusing on copying the native speaker's intonation and rhythm.

Shadowing is quite the workout at first, and it remains a good method to build our mouth muscles as we encounter more language to mimic. If you are interested in things like intonation, pronunciation, speaking confidence, and accent reduction, this is the technique for you. It's also challenging and incredibly fun.

Before or after each Shadowing exercise, it's recommended to check where the low and high pitches are located using the Suzuki-kun tool's approximation. Listen very carefully to the native speakers again and see if you can pick up the high and low pitches. They can be very subtle at first, but these pitches are important to natural sounding Japanese.

Unfortunately, this exercise can only be done with video and audio Japanese sources, so written materials will be left out. There are methods to get native Japanese speakers to record such lines, but they are highly inconvenient and are generally not worth the time and money to acquire. Text-to-speech robots are not accurate enough yet to imitate proper intonation, so I do not recommend Shadowing after them.

How To Setup

When you download, install, and open up Anki, click 'Create Deck' and name it whatever you like. We will only need one deck for now, as all four of our flashcard types will go into this deck. Click 'Add' at the top and then click 'Basic' at the top of the new window. By default, you should see four card types.

THE ORIGINAL FOUR CARD TYPES IN ANKI

Let's add Production, Listening, and Shadowing cards. Creating card types for each one takes seconds and allows for easy reference and organization if we ever wish to change something in bulk. If you click "Manage", you can delete the unnecessary cards and keep "Cloze". Next, click "Add" and select "Add:Basic" and rename it to "Production". Repeat this process for "Listening" and "Shadowing."

After that, you will need to install an add-on called "AwesomeTTS". It offers multiple free Text to Speech services that we can integrate into Anki. With a simple install and Anki reboot, we can simply paste the word or sentence into the 'Front' or 'Back' box, highlight it, and click the speaker icon from the add-on to quickly generate the audio in seconds.

Awesome TTS:
https://ankiweb.net/shared/info/301952613

AwesomeTTS will allow us to do the Listening and Shadowing card types by placing these files into the 'Front' box. We can also add extra audio reinforcement to our Production and Cloze cards by placing these files in the 'Back' box. When these exercises appear during Anki review sessions, the sound file will automatically play by default, but you can replay the sound file when needed by pressing the 'R' button on your keyboard.

Some Text to Speech services can sometimes create slightly muddled audio files, but 'VoiceText' and 'Oddcast' seem to be the most reliable and easiest to understand. And in case AwesomeTTS is ever removed for any reason, the internet provides multiple free Text to Speech services that can be used as a replacement.

Finally, the cards are reviewed in the order that they are made by default, but shuffling the cards is strongly recommended. Otherwise, the same words and contexts will be clumped together in consecutive exercises, and after the first card, we will simply be testing our short-term memory rather than long-term memory.

To shuffle the cards, open Anki and click on the gear to the right of your deck and select 'Options'. Click the 'New cards' tab, look for 'Order', and select 'Show new cards in random order'. If there is ever a time you would like to reshuffle the deck for whatever reason, select 'Show new cards in order added', press OK, select 'Show new cards in random order' again, and press OK again.

Inserting Images and Audio

Images and audio from instructional and native materials aren't required, but they are a means to create a stronger link from what we are reviewing inside Anki to what we are reading and listening to every day. The original image and audio can make Anki sessions much more meaningful and memorable, and your efforts here will be rewarded.

For instance, still images from videos are super easy to insert. While the video is on the screen and paused at the appropriate moment, press the 'PrtSc' button (Command + Shift + 3 for Macs) on your keyboard. Then, you will need to open up a basic image editing program like Paint in Windows (Paintbrush for Macs) and crop the image to your liking before saving it. When adding cards to Anki, make sure the cursor is in the 'Front' text box, and click the paperclip icon to add your image or audio.

Coursebooks and textbooks provide easy access to native speaker recordings via CD, but inserting audio from native materials is a little more difficult. For educational purposes, you will need to obtain the original audio or video source.

There are of course many ways to create the audio clips you want. I found the free audio editing program Audacity (*http://www.audacityteam.org*) to work well enough.

Subs2srs (*http://subs2srs.sourceforge.net*) offers an additional option that allows you to easily turn entire anime episodes into Anki decks. This even includes the original images and audio files. The downside is, however, all the cards will become basic reading and translation exercises.

Example Context

To demonstrate these exercises in action, let's look at an example sentence, break it down, and see what exercises we can create to master any potentially new language here.

Example Sentence:

有名な作家と対談してみたい。

Translation:

I want to interview a famous author.

Quick Breakdown:

有名 --- famous

な --- This attaches to 有名 so that we can attach it to a noun (e.g. author).

作家 --- author

と --- This particle is used when an action (e.g. the interviewing) is done with somebody or something else (e.g. a famous author).

対談 --- interview / talk / conversation

してみたい --- want to try

Anki Practice Exercises:

Here's just one out of many possible combinations of Anki exercises that you could make from this sentence:

---

an author

PRODUCTION # 1: 作家が

Eric Bodnar

interview / talk / discussion

PRODUCTION # 2: **対談が**

55

a famous author

PRODUCTION # 3: 有名な作家が

Eric Bodnar

I want to interview / talk with

PRODUCTION # 4: 対談してみたい

an interview with an author

PRODUCTION # 5: 作家と対談が

Eric Bodnar

有名な{...}家と対談してみたい

CLOZE # 1: 作

有名な作{...}と対談してみたい

CLOZE # 2: 家

有名な作家と{...}談してみたい

CLOZE # 3: 対

有名な作家と対{...}してみたい

CLOZE # 4: 談

Eric Bodnar

作家が

(audio file)

LISTENING # 1: an author

対談が

(audio file)

LISTENING # 2: interview / talk / discussion

有名な作家が

(audio file)

LISTENING # 3: a famous author

対談してみたい
(audio file)

LISTENING # 4: I want to interview / talk with

作家と対談が

(audio file)

LISTENING # 5: an interview with an author

SHADOWING # 1: with no text

I want to interview a famous author.

SHADOWING # 2: with English translation

有名な作家と対談してみたい。

SHADOWING # 3: with Japanese transcription

How to Master Your Textbook

Here is just one possible way you could apply these Anki exercises to master your initial Japanese coursebook. For new vocabulary words and set phrases, create one Production and one Listening card.

Verb conjugation tables can be tackled with Production and Listening exercises. There is no need to make these cards for every possible conjugation and verb. That wouldn't be easy or fun. Start with just three, four, or five verbs for now. Focus only on the most commonly used forms like the polite form (-ます), the negative form (-ない), the past form (-んだ/-た/-った/-かった), and the passive form (-せる). Rather than make one Production and one Listening for every form, split the conjugations between the two exercises to save time. You can always make more as you learn new verbs.

For every major grammar point or topic covered, grab three, four, or five sentences and make one Listening card for each. You can use Cloze cards as well to test for kanji, vocabulary, and correct grammar usage if you think there is enough context to make the answer clear and unambiguous.

Monologues, dialogues, and long passages found in textbooks are perfect for Cloze as well as Shadowing exercises. These scenarios provide good opportunities to speak alongside a native speaker and to try to keep up with their intonation and speed to the best of our ability. Use Production, Cloze, and Listening as you see fit to breakdown all the new vocabulary, phrases, and grammar in these larger contexts. The Shadowing cards may be few and far in between during review sessions, but you can use these gigantic gaps to gauge your personal progress as you eventually encounter each one.

A high amount of Production and Listening, a moderate amount of Cloze, and a low amount of Shadowing has worked well for me in the past, but feel free to experiment with the ratio. You can also experiment with different sources of Japanese to create exercises with as you will see in the next chapter.

10,000 PAGES OF MANGA

Back in Chapter Two, we covered how you can learn Japanese by listening to native materials starting from day one, so now the challenge lies in figuring out how to get yourself to read more Japanese every day. This chapter will focus on why you should read Japanese every day and techniques you can use to ease into reading when it is so overwhelmingly difficult at first.

After studying comes to an end for the day, why read when you can just keep listening for hours on end? For starters, it will help you to quickly convert more of that incomprehensible stream of Japanese gibberish into a language you can understand. Secondly, some of the world's most skilled polyglots like Alexander Arguelles, Luca Lampariello, and Steve Kaufmann are major advocates of reading as a means to learn foreign languages. Finally, reading helps you to build an even wider range of vocabulary while also providing another fun and holistic way to learn and practice Japanese.

Reading gives you more activities you can do to keep engaged in learning and ultimately living through Japanese for hours every day. For example, you could switch between watching one anime series, reading another manga series, watching some live streaming video in Japanese, and doing some lighter reading in a Japanese video game all in a single day.

Reading native Japanese materials is tremendously slow and difficult as a beginner, so when exactly should you get started? As soon as possible is ideal if you're looking to get really good at Japanese within a few years. You should start whenever reading and writing kana is no longer a major obstacle to you. This could take two to three weeks or more depending on how fast you are looking to learn. The more you expose yourself to written Japanese the better. The more early attempts at reading you make, the faster you will learn.

There is no need to worry about kanji in the early stages of reading. You can find plenty of reading material that is written with furigana (smaller kana written above kanji to indicate its pronunciation) or in kana only. This includes a nearly unlimited supply of shounen and shoujo manga. This also includes playing games like *Pokémon* which will give you tons of reading practice.

But if you play something like *Pokémon* in Japanese, do you stop to look up every new word? When do you just relax and play the game? It can be completely overwhelming at first. And within 20 minutes of trying to read anything in the beginner stages, you can be left completely drained and discouraged. This is where smart language learning techniques and strategies can come in handy.

Intensive vs. Extensive Reading

To answer this question, we need to understand the difference between intensive and extensive reading. In intensive reading, the goal is to break down and look up every single new word and grammar point in a selected reading of somewhat shorter length. This kind of reading is only intended to last around 20-45 minutes. If you have ever taken a foreign language class, chances are that you are familiar with intensive reading.

In extensive reading, however, the goal is to read for pleasure and for longer periods of time while relying on context alone to learn new words. You can only study a small amount of pages before your mind starts giving out, but when you read a text that is very easy for your level, you can read a much larger quantity of pages for several hours before stopping.

Unfortunately, the problem is that it's very tough to find extensive reading materials for your level when you are in the beginner and intermediate stages. It's estimated that you need 98% comprehension of a text before you are able to do true extensive reading.

This chapter will cover intensive reading strategies while the last chapter will explore how to make extensive reading more accessible in the beginning and intermediate levels. But in general, it's easier to start your day with 45-90 minutes of study and Anki review time, move on to intensive reading and listening, and finish with extensive reading and listening.

And yes, you read that right. Intensive and extensive listening exist as well. Listening intensively to a single anime episode while on the lookout for high frequency words is an example of intensive listening. The final chapter will also cover extensive listening.

Why Manga Is the Perfect Start

Of course, you may choose any material to start intensively reading with, but here are some reasons why you may want to consider starting with manga first. Not only is a good manga story infinitely more interesting than your average newspaper article or short story, it's also much easier to clearly track and see your progress.

Newspaper articles and short stories are popular first reading choices for language learners, but it can be somewhat hard to stay consistent in reading these types of traditional reading materials every day. After a few weeks or months, it can seem like an endless stream of Japanese to work through. This is because news articles and short stories aren't connected most of the time. There's no overarching story driving you to read until the very end to find out what happens.

With manga, however, the end of a chapter signifies both the progress you have made and also adds a bit of overall plot progression as well. Sometimes, you even get a new surprise twist! It's much harder to get these feelings with a string of unrelated newspaper articles or short stories.

Manga also tends to be a very light read. You have beautifully drawn images to guide you and give you more context. You can turn pages relatively quickly compared to other written materials. And each time you turn the page, it sends your brain a small message that you are making progress!

Use each page, chapter, volume, and series to track that progress because you are going to need it. Reading a manga chapter is a lot more exhausting than watching an episode of anime. It may even help to set an initial goal to work towards like 10,000 pages of manga within a year or two. There's no deep meaning behind this number of manga pages, but it's an example of a clear and measurable goal that can help to keep you reading every day without fail.

The first chapters and volumes will be very slow at first. Prepare yourself. It will be labor intensive. No matter what series you choose to start with, there will be a ton of words that you have never seen or heard before. It's very likely that you will have to go through your first series pretty heavily with a dictionary or English translation in order to understand what's happening in the story.

That's why I highly recommend buying actual physical copies of Japanese manga for intensive reading. It gets you away from all the distractions that come with reading at the computer. Not only is it an incredible feeling to possess the real thing in your hands, you can also be at your highest level of concentration while working your way through. Flipping through real pages is all the more satisfying and beats clicking through internet pages anytime. It's very much worth the money to buy your first series off of eBay.

Measuring your progress towards 10,000 pages is much more straightforward with physical books. It makes it a little bit simpler when adding up page numbers, and it makes your progress both tangible and visible. Personally, I have never been much of a collector of anything, but my mind changed shortly after finally taking the plunge and buying my first manga series.

The Rule of Two

As an alternative, you may choose to do intensive reading with visual novels, video games, or even anime. With the help of Japanese subtitles found on *http://kitsunekko.net* and on Netflix, you can turn almost any anime or Japanese TV show into both an intensive reading and listening activity. The best part is that it's possible to learn much more than just words without ever stopping the video once. You don't need to go through entire episodes line by line from start to finish to effectively learn from them.

Let's now revisit the system discussed in the first chapter but this time go into more detail. Immerse yourself in any native Japanese material of your choosing without English subtitles or translations for roughly 20 minutes. As you carefully read, watch, and listen, be on the lookout for the unknown words that you have seen or heard multiple times. Quickly write down the unknown words that are repeated two or more times and continue without stopping the reading, video, or audio. Include the page numbers, video times, audio track times, and screenshots for reference later.

In case the video materials like anime, feel free to jot down a few crucial moments that you greatly desire to understand as well. After the episode ends or approximately 20 minutes have passed, you will have a list of high frequency words and moments of high interest to you. Go through your list item by item using the Japanese subtitle files to learn as much as you can. Find each line for each item on your list and break down its meaning using online dictionaries, grammar resources, and even the English subtitles.

In the case of reading native Japanese materials like manga, you may read past the 20 minute mark for however long you would like. Keep going until you find yourself growing continually bored or mentally fatigued. This is usually the best place to stop.

While reading, you may use a dictionary to look up as many words and kanji as you need. At the same time, it's not necessary to look up every single unknown word and kanji, so go at whatever pace feels most comfortable to you. If it proves to be more convenient, you could even check the English translation after every page rather than the dictionary after every new word. As long as you are engaging the Japanese text and trying to understand it, feel free to use the English translation however you like.

After the reading has come to an end whether through manga, Japanese subtitle files, or elsewhere, you will have identified and learned the meaning behind the high frequency words and the lines of dialogue they came from. Pick zero, one, or two of what you feel are the most important passages to practice and create Anki cards for them. One passage can be either a single sentence, a few sentences, or even brief dialogues (two to three lines).

But why pick just one or two passages and no more? I suggest setting this kind of rule to advocate spending less time reviewing with Anki so that you can make more time for more reading and listening to native Japanese. Remember that Anki is not the only way to review.

If all these new words, kanji, and grammar structures are so important, they will show up again somewhere later. Encountering new words, phrases, and grammar points from multiple contexts is how we build upon our understanding of how to use them. It also makes them harder to forget each time we re-learn them.

For this reason, we can even pick zero passages to practice with Anki to go straight back to reading, listening, and learning. You may want to save Anki for the toughest words and sentence structures that you have looked up over and over and still have trouble understanding. When it comes to how much or how little Anki to use, the choice is yours.

Forget the Rest!

While you're looking up mostly everything that is new to you in intensive reading, I wouldn't recommend going through each entire subtitle file from start to finish. Watching an episode of an anime or a drama with no subtitles from start to finish is already an intensive listening activity as is. Learn what you can each episode and move on when you can no longer stay focused.

Listen, watch, and read as you normally do in English. Watch videos and read materials just once and no more. Don't watch the same video, movie, or TV episode over and over until you break down everything from it for the sake of learning. It can be maddening after your third or fourth viewing. What might be more fun is exploring the near endless amount of native Japanese material available. Learning just a few lines of dialogue from each episode is enough to move on to the next one.

That last line is so vital to making all of this learning fun, so I would like to repeat just once more. Learning just a few words or lines of dialogue from each episode is enough to move on to the next one.

Reading Subtitle Files

In order to read the Japanese subtitle files from kitsunekko.net, you will need a free program called Aegisub (*http://www.aegisub.org*). The times in the video and subtitle file will most likely be out of sync, so it may take a minute or two to locate the lines that you want to learn. Why not think of this search time as training your Japanese eyes and ears to become stronger? Alternatively, you can use Subs2srs if you would like.

Let's find the line from this moment from the first episode of *Dragon Ball Super*.

DRAGON BALL SUPER EPISODE 1

After a minute or two of reading and listening, I have found it!

DRAGON BALL SUPER EPISODE 1 JAPANESE SUBTITLE FILE

Learning Kanji in the Wild

Let printed Japanese be no obstacle to you. You can identify unknown words and kanji through furigana, and if no furigana is present, you can use a few tricks to identify unknown kanji and words. This is where you will need some initial kanji training. If you can recognize just one of the radicals used, you can use an online dictionary like *http://jisho.org* to search for the correct kanji. If you know how many strokes make up the new character, this will aid you all the more. If you can guess the stroke order correctly, you can search by drawing them in the dictionary.

Ultimately, the order in which you learn the kanji does not matter. Let kanji resources such as "Remembering the Kanji" (RTK) be servants and not masters. Learn as many as you can before you get bored of these resources, and then, just start learning kanji in the wild.

For example, we can use free website Kanji Koohii (*www.kanji.koohii.com*) to find mnemonic stories for any of the 3000 kanji covered by RTK. Simply copy and paste any unknown kanji to you, and you will find a high-quality collection of user-submitted mnemonic stories that range from highly creative to silly and absurd. You can use their stories, alter them if needed, and save them to your account. Sometimes other users will provide just the right story that is unforgettable.

Unfortunately, these mnemonic stories do not contain the Japanese readings of the kanji, so they must be learned elsewhere. So how do you learn to read them aloud as the Japanese can do so effortlessly?

I still clearly remember being overwhelmed when trying to read and pronounce the kanji during my first year, but those reading problems disappeared when I gradually realized a more practical way to learn them. Don't try to learn the readings of each individual kanji. Focus on learning vocabulary instead. Since the readings are dependent upon the vocabulary the kanji is used in, you'll automatically learn the readings as they come up in learning new vocabulary.

Let's look at an example with the kanji 行 meaning "go". It's a very basic kanji, but it's notorious for having so many different readings. If you looked it up in the dictionary, you might get a headache when you see the ten or more potential readings it has. Since the vocabulary determines which kanji reading is used, what good is this information besides scaring students away? Screw those readings! They are arbitrary and useless to memorize.

Start with just the one reading that is tied to the vocabulary word that you are learning and ignore the rest. Let's say the word 行く meaning "to go" came up while reading. If you have been learning Japanese for more than a week, you probably already know this word, so just focus on your mnemonic story to help you write it from memory and its one reading here (い) when used in the verb 行く.

Deal with the other readings as you encounter them in future passages. Perhaps a month later you may find 旅行 meaning "travel" in one of your passages. A quick dictionary check will tell you that 行 is pronounced as "コウ" in this case. As you keep mining sentences over weeks, months, and years, you'll find 行 read as "コウ" in many other two kanji compound words like 銀行 and 急行. These "い" and "コウ" readings are what you will see most of the time, and you will eventually learn the other readings whenever they surface in whatever Japanese material you immerse yourself in.

Context is king when it comes to remembering kanji, vocabulary, and grammar. When we learn kanji through the context of new vocabulary and learn new vocabulary through an even larger context like dialogue from an anime, all this information becomes much more memorable and meaningful.

Choose Easy

If you decide to review one or two passages using Anki, let's make sure that they are appropriate for your level. If you select contexts with four or more unknown words altogether, it's still very much possible to break down all the vocabulary, grammar, and kanji. Yet when these difficult passages are repeatedly selected for Anki, too many new words, phrases, and grammar points can make the review process slow-paced and tedious.

These types of passages can lead to frustrating Anki exercises. During a Cloze exercise, you won't be able to figure out the missing word or kanji if there are too many unfamiliar words in the context. And for the same reason, Listening exercises won't be helpful nor effective. Your tongue will also seemingly freeze up while Shadowing when the difficulty bar is set too high. These kinds of exercises can cause your interest to wane and take the enjoyment out of Anki reviews.

Choosing easy can make learning so much more fun and even addictive. Choosing contexts with just one, two, or three new words allows learning to happen seemingly at a faster pace. When the level of the challenge before us is at just the right level, we can enter a flow-like state where learning becomes much more pleasurable and satisfying.

Divide and Conquer

In the end, you may use the Anki exercises any way that you wish, but here is one way to dissect new material. New words, phrases, and verb conjugations get one Production and one Listening card. New or still unfamiliar kanji get one Cloze card. New vocabulary and phrases also get one Cloze card for each kanji they contain. And Shadowing gets three cards (Blind Shadowing, Shadowing with English text, and Shadowing with Japanese text).

CONSISTENCY, ROUTINE, AND HABIT

This final chapter is perhaps the most important one contained in this book. It's a call to action. It asks you the reader to stop passively reading along and to start taking action. If you don't take action every day towards learning Japanese and doing activities in Japanese, fluency will remain an enigma and forever be outside of your reach. If you want to be really good at Japanese, you have to make it a major part of your daily life. Taking steps every single day towards what you desire the most is how you create and maintain new habits.

When it comes to taking action towards creating new habits, however, there is a universal truth that we must face. If it does not get scheduled, it does not get done. We must decide on —and then commit to —a routine that we will follow every day, as faithfully as we can. Otherwise, lesser tasks and distractions sneak in, and the age-old excuse of "I couldn't find the time..." starts coming out of our mouths. That classic excuse signals that we never took the next step to set up a specific time and place.

In this last chapter, we will explore ideas regarding language learning routines you can use starting right now to speed up the rate at which you learn Japanese. We will also take a look at how you can incorporate extensive reading and listening into your schedule no matter what level of Japanese you are currently at.

Studying in general, which includes the Anki exercises, tends to require the most focus of all, so it's highly recommended to knock it out as early as possible each day. Each morning before school or work or even right afterward is ideal while you have the most energy and momentum to get the hardest part done. 45 to 90 minutes is all you need here.

Start with 10/10 Sessions

Our next order of business is to make a few small adjustments to Anki's schedule so that you aren't stuck reviewing cards for more than two hours every day.

Anki review sessions involve doing new cards (color coded blue in Anki) and review cards (color coded green in Anki). New cards are exercises that have been created but not yet seen during review sessions. Review cards have been viewed at least once before. So, 10/10 refers to doing an Anki session with 10 new cards and 10 review cards, or in other words, 20 exercises in total.

In Anki, you can set the number of exercises to be completed per day to 10/10 or whatever numbers you would like. This can easily be done by opening Anki, clicking on the gear to the right of your deck, and selecting 'Options'. Set 'New cards/day' to 10, and then click the 'Reviews' tab and set 'Maximum reviews/day' to 10.

100 "Maximum reviews/day" is the current default setting in Anki at the time of writing this book, but if you keep this setting, Anki review sessions alone can quickly start exceeding 90 minutes daily when the reviews begin to pile up. This does not include the time it takes to create cards from new material.

On a more personal note, I can say the following with a high amount of confidence. Pushing myself to do 50+ Anki cards every day was one of the largest factors that led to my eventual burnout with learning Korean.

The starting recommendation is set to 10/10 review sessions, and caution is advised if you would like to increase those numbers. If you want to incorporate more Anki reviews, a larger number such as 20/20 could potentially be done if broken into two or more smaller sessions throughout the day. Doing such a large number every day will be a tremendously difficult habit to maintain, but if you are feeling particularly motivated to do more Anki on certain days, go for it.

Doing a needlessly high amount of Anki cards day after day can be more detrimental than helpful. More Anki does not mean more learning and progress if it causes your internal motivation meter to plummet and approach zero. Stop training for the Agony Olympics with hellish ultra-marathons of Anki reviews.

You will do exponentially more Anki cards just by doing small sessions consistently as a habit. To build this consistency with Anki, keep sessions under an hour and don't force yourself to do more for the sake of faster progress. Stop right before you get bored and keep yourself hungry for the next session.

Start with 5/5 sessions if you have trouble focusing during 10/10 sessions. Train to grow stronger in both Japanese proficiency and your ability to focus deeply. If you have a habit of waking up and going straight to social media in the morning, chances are that you will have great difficulty in trying to maintain focus while studying, reading, or listening to raw Japanese. Consider starting your day with morning walks, uplifting messages, and inspirational audiobooks to draw your focus away from all the distractions of the world so that you can focus within your inner world.

Extensive Reading and Listening

Your brain can be sapped after 45-90 minutes of study and Anki reviews, but if you stopped at this point, you would be forgetting a very important piece to gaining fluency. And that is the thousands and thousands of hours of reading and listening to native Japanese. This includes both the intensive and extensive varieties.

Choosing which old hobbies and activities to sacrifice to make time for more Japanese is a difficult choice, but it's much easier to start with the dead times of the day or what is also known as downtime. Turn this downtime into "up-time" by taking a manga book to read wherever you go. Time spent walking, biking, and driving can be turned into listening time by making sure your mobile device is stocked with hours of Japanese entertainment to listen to.

True extensive reading is extremely difficult to get into as a beginner or intermediate learner, but video games offer one way to making reading more accessible no matter what level you are at. Although you can do intensive reading with video games as well, they are perfect for extensive reading.

Just like watching anime with no subtitles for the first time, start with a game that you have seen or played before. Many people have played *Pokémon* at one point or another, so that may be where you want to start. If you are a fan of old-school RPGs, take this time to revisit the classics: *Super Mario RPG*, *Chrono Trigger*, and *Final Fantasy VI*.

When you already know the premise of the game, you can casually read through the text and dialogue while using context to decipher new words along the way. Try to keep your dictionary use as minimal as possible. Remember that extensive reading should be very easy so that you can do it for hours at a time, and constantly going to the dictionary can really put a damper on that. Use in-game progress and the number of games you complete to track your extensive reading progress.

Extensive listening, however, is as simple as choosing to follow more Japanese shows than you follow in English. Binge watching a few anime series will not turn you into a weeb. In fact, it's quite fun and rewarding. It will even help to get you closer and closer to understanding everything in realistic Japanese dramas, TV shows, and movies.

You pick something to watch and press play. That's it. There's no need to listen for the high frequency words here. You just listen purely for pleasure. Listen when you are in need of a break or when you are tired at the end of the day. More listening equals more practice, and you will even occasionally learn a thing or two through context alone. The parts you can't understand help motivate you to come back the next day ready to learn more.

This habit of immersing yourself in native Japanese should take precedence over your old hobbies if you really want to reach an advanced or even near-native levels within a few years. You need to train your eyes and ears daily and put in every hour and minute that you can.

Going complete immersion in your home environment is not required for fluency, but either way you'll see significantly more satisfying results when you start living primarily through Japanese. Whether or not you are looking to go full immersion, it would still be wise to keep your study and Anki sessions under 90 minutes or so. There comes a point in time during each day where you have to stop studying and starting living the language!

Experiment by making your own Japanese schedules to suit your personal needs. Test your own ideas and see what brings the most learning and enjoyment to your program. You could start with intensive reading and listening first and move on to extensive reading and listening later in the day. Or you could even try switching between intensive and extensive activities to give yourself a break when needed.

Lang-8, Italki, and HelloTalk

Output practice could also fill in for some of this time in your schedule. Let's look at three different ways to get in contact with native speakers and receive corrections.

Lang-8 *(http://lang-8.com)* is a free language exchange website where users make posts in the language that they wish to practice. You receive corrections in exchange for correcting other people's posts in your native language. Users can write about anything. You can write about what has been on your mind all day or even specific topics that you are interested in. When you correct other people's posts, corrections for your entries come within hours.

In terms of time and money, Lang-8 may be the most effective way of receiving corrections. It is very convenient to visit the page at any time, write for 10-20 minutes, make a few easy corrections for other users, and leave to go about your day. Later during the same day or even the next day, you can return to find the corrections.

If you are willing to pay a few dollars a session to speak with tutors face to face, Italki *(https://www.italki.com)* may be the better alternative. In order to use Italki, you will need to search for a teacher of your liking, schedule for an available time slot, and log on to Skype *(https://www.skype.com)*. Face-to-face conversation and tutoring does have its advantages, so it may be worth the price to you.

HelloTalk *(https://www.hellotalk.com)* is a highly popular app that has opened new possibilities for language exchange through texting. Most language learners rate this app very positively, as it is possibly the most convenient way to connect directly with native speakers of almost any language. It's a great platform to start organic conversations with Japanese people. Make new Japanese friends as you talk in each other's native language and also receive corrections along the way. Texting certainly takes the pressure off of face to face conversations in meeting new people, so this may be the choice for you.

Anki Is Good, But...

Feel free to take as much time off from studying and Anki to go out and live the language! In fact, whenever you feel that you are well into the intermediate stages of learning Japanese, I recommend stopping all studying and Anki use all together. When you have a vocabulary of several thousand words, a good grasp of pitch accent and pronunciation, and a solid foundation in grammar and kanji, studying and Anki reviews are no longer necessary.

Anki is great in the beginner and early intermediate stages for internalizing the basics of Japanese, but in the end, it's not the most efficient when it comes to building vocabulary and overall language competency. If you try putting every new word you learn into Anki, it will slow down your reading and listening to a snail's pace. Even if you were to do just an hour of Anki reviews a day, it can be infinitely more fun to spend that hour reviewing those thousands of words through more reading and listening to native Japanese materials.

I never realized this truth in my four years of hardcore studying Korean, and I even relied too heavily on Anki in my early years of learning Japanese. It was not until I decided to start reading manga for not just 20 minutes here and there but hours every single day that I realized that reading and listening to native materials was an overall more effective review strategy than Anki.

You get really good not by studying a few hundred pages but by reading thousands of pages. That's how you win the game. When you finally stop studying, you start to feel that you're not just learning the language anymore but you're also truly living it.

These last two chapters have demonstrated just a few ways on how to track your language learning progress without Anki. It can be by means of counting physical manga pages and volumes or even feeling your overall Japanese ability level up as you make progress in video games. You may also want to keep a list of anime episodes and series you have watched and completed without subtitles.

It might sound unnecessary and even a little bit silly, but these small things can and do make you feel that you are on the right track towards fluency. That feeling is what gets you to come back every day and be more than willing to put in the hours.

The End

Thank you so much for taking the time to read my book! If you enjoyed the book, please take a minute to review it now on Amazon. Even a one or two line review will really help support me and help other people find their way to this book.

Also, be sure to visit my YouTube channel Fluent Japanese From Anime for more information, examples, updates, and even lessons using the system covered in this book.

(www.youtube.com/c/fluentjapanesefromanime)

Appendix: Links and Resources

Japanese subtitles for anime:
http://kitsunekko.net

Anki:
www.ankisrs.net

Goldlist Method:
https://huliganov.tv/goldlist-eu

Jisho (English-Japanese dictionary):
http://jisho.org

Niconico (fun Japanese video sharing website):
http://www.nicovideo.jp

OPENREC.tv (video game live streaming website):
https://www.openrec.tv

Learn ALL Hiragana in 1 Hour —How to Write and Read Japanese:
https://www.youtube.com/watch?v=6p9Il_j0zjc

Suzuki-kun (Japanese pitch accent tool):
http://www.gavo.t.u-tokyo.ac.jp/ojad/eng/phrasing/index

Dogen's Japanese Phonetics Series:
https://www.patreon.com/dogen

Shadowing Step by Step by Alexander Arguelles:
https://www.youtube.com/watch?v=130bOvRpt24

AwesomeTTS (text to speech add-on for Anki):
https://ankiweb.net/shared/info/301952613

Audacity (for extracting audio from video):
http://www.audacityteam.org

Subs2srs (turn any anime episode into a Anki deck):
http://subs2srs.sourceforge.net

Aegisub (to open and read subtitle files):
http://www.aegisub.org

Kanji Koohii (for kanji mnemonic stories):
www.kanji.koohii.com

Lang-8:
http://lang-8.com

Italki:
https://www.italki.com

HelloTalk:
https://www.hellotalk.com